BOOK *of* HOURS

BOOK *of* HOURS

Kevin Young

ALFRED A. KNOPF
New York
2014

THIS IS A BORZOI BOOK
PUBLISHED BY ALFRED A. KNOPF

www.aaknopf.com/poetry

Knopf, Borzoi Books, and the colophon are registered
trademarks of Random House, LLC

Library of Congress Cataloging-in-Publication Data
Young, Kevin.
[Poems. Selections]
Book of Hours / by Kevin Young. —First Edition.
pages   cm
Poems.
ISBN 978-0-307-27224-9
I. Title.
PS3575.O798B66   2014
811'.54—dc23   2013019328

Front-of-jacket image: CSA Images/
B&W Engrave Ink Collection/Vetta/Getty Images
Jacket design by Kelly Blair

Manufactured in the United States of America
First Edition

for Addie & Mack

GO SWEETLY
KNOW I LOVE YOU

Gods do not answer letters.
—JOHN UPDIKE
on baseball player Ted Williams

When the finger of God appears,
it's usually the wrong finger.
—CHARLES WRIGHT

Lord Lord
Lord Lord Lord.
—BLIND WILLIE MCTELL

Contents

(CONFIRMATION)

(x)

BOOK *of* HOURS

Obsequies

for my father
1942–2004

Dark dirigible,
    filled with sorrow,
on fire.

*

Sleep's a distant
    love—no pillow cool
enough, or soft.

*

    Morning & memory
floods the room
    like light—can sun
be awful?
    Can the mind?

*

Laundry
    like a prayer—
weekly, or more,
    & endless.

*

Doubt keeps a kind
    of faith, is belief
without a word
    for what

*

it knows—
    plenty
for what we don't.

*

At night I count
not the stars
    but the dark.

*

(DOMESDAY BOOK)

We stare into somewhere
the sun

hasn't been

We stare where
the sun's no longer

Elegy, Father's Day

From above, baseball diamonds look
even more beautiful, the pitcher's mound

a bright cataract.
The river wavers

its own way—see
where once it snaked.

Shine me like a light.

Ladies & Gentlemen, we are flying
just above turbulence.

The roads like centipedes,
their flailing feet.

How many, thousands,
to fall.

Below, parcels & acres blur
like family plots.

(9)

100 knots.

Cities bright
in the blinding dawn.

We make good time—

roads like scars
in the green—

grids of an earth
too soon we'll meet.

Bereavement

Behind his house, my father's dogs
sleep in kennels, beautiful,
he built just for them.

They do not bark.
Do they know he is dead?
They wag their tails

& head. They beg
& are fed.
Their grief is colossal

& forgetful.
Each day they wake
seeking his voice,

their names.
By dusk they seem
to unremember everything—

to them even hunger
is a game. For that, I envy.
For that, I cannot bear to watch them

pacing their cage. I try to remember
they love best confined space
to feel safe. Each day

a saint comes by to feed the pair
& I draw closer
the shades.

I've begun to think of them
as my father's other sons,
as kin. Brothers-in-paw.

My eyes each day thaw.
One day the water cuts off.
Then back on.

They are outside dogs—
which is to say, healthy
& victorious, purposeful

& one giant muscle
like the heart. Dad taught
them not to bark, to point

out their prey. To stay.
Were they there that day?
They call me

like witnesses & will not say.
I ask for their care
& their carelessness—

wish of them forgiveness.
I must give them away.
I must find for them homes,

sleep restless in his.
All night I expect they pace
as I do, each dog like an eye

roaming with the dead
beneath an unlocked lid.

Act Now & Save

It's a wonder the world
keeps its whirling—

How I've waited
without a word—

Staring where
the sun's no longer—

You gone
into ether, wherever

You want
to call it. Soon

Sun won't fight
off the cold

But today warm
even in the rain.

Whatever the well
you want me

To fall down I will—

Meet me by the deepest
part of the river

And we'll drown together
wading out past

All care, beyond even
the shore's hollers.

Effects

It was a ghost
        town, a town
not of the dead

but the deserted—
        once thriving—a hospital
named not for a saint

nor Women & Children—
        whoever's first—but for the city
where you'd been flown

for now. The help desk
        was no help. You
were somewhere

else, already your body lost
        in the basement dark,
where, if you had eyes

left, they soon would adjust   (13)
        & you could see.
The last to see you

being helped
        to breathe
was your friend the Judge

I asked over the phone
        to look in on you
in your next-

to-last room, to make sure
        the rehearsed nurse
told the truth. Your brain

dead, body a machine—
It's bad,
he said, acting

as my eyes. Yours
        I soon would give—
flown here to retrieve

your effects
        from a chilly teller,
this banker of bodies.

Well below
        in the morgue, the walls
of the dead in their safe

deposit boxes—
        your wallet handed back
signed for, unspent. What

(14)   was left. The lobby
        like a cathedral bombed
but whose rose

window still shone—
        me a prisoner released
too early, on furlough,

with nowheres
        to go. Outside
strangely spring

but cold—on break,
     nurses in their abstract
expressionist shirts

huddled & shared
     cigarettes, exhaling
thick halos of smoke.

Rue

Strange how you keep on
  dying—not once
then over

& done with—or for—
  if not every day
anymore, each morning

a sabbath of sundering,
  then hours still arrive
I realize nothing

can beg you back—
  nor return to us days
without harm, heaven

only an idea. Hell not yet
  that week
I couldn't bear to sleep

in your half-life house
  & my future
wife & I stayed

at the Worst
  Western, the phone
ringing early, & late,

too late. I'd wake

& you'd be there, gone—
  retreating
to the bleak bathroom

& its heat lamp, perched
       on the edge
of the empty tub, I'd try

not to write.
       How terrible
to have to pick up

the pen, helpless
       to it, your death
not yet

a habit & try to say
       something other than
never, or *hereafter,*

to praise among the tile—
       not your dying—
but having

been alive. The pale bathroom   (17)

whose light burnt on, red
       as a darkroom,
ticking down—

your eulogy dashed out
       among the tiny
broken soap, each day

shrinking, slivered
       in our hands. Come late
afternoon, the distant, wet slaps

of children poolside
crying out
in laughter—their muffled

watery shrieks echoing after.

Bereavement Fare

Nothing fair about it—

Heaven on
the layaway plan.

Huge interest.

Now the world's
only noun—

A weather
no map dare measure.

Mercy

On line for the plane
a woman carried her heart
on her lap & I thought

could it be yours
she held tight? It wasn't
her heart yet

of course, was her future
heart, I guess, soon
inside her beating

after being dead
on the table, a minute
or two, during surgery

in a hospital named Mercy.
For now, wheeled
alongside her, her almost

(20)   heart sat labeled
& tucked in its red chest
of ice. I thought

I could be her
holding you, hoping
there was enough life left in you

to help me
again breathe.
I knew full well

you were not there,
father, that it was your liver
lifted out of you

& set like a bloody stone
inside somebody
else to save. After being

checked for danger, just
beyond the glass doors,
I watched

a farmer father
& mother send off
their plaid son

the first time he'd flown,
everyone wiping their eyes
& waving.

Near Miss

Not the storm.

Not the light
that keeps

me awake
but the noise.

Instruments now
are so good they know

a hurricane far
before it starts. Even

winds have names. Mine's
not worth mentioning—

more of a sound
these days.

Old man, Sir—
who, alone, in the room

with your body lying
in state

I saluted—

it is forgetting, not watery
memory, that scares me.

All
is forgiven, even

the notion of anything
left to forgive.

Not the storm
but the calm

that slays me.

Grief

In the night I brush
my teeth with a razor

Solace

All I craved
    day after he died
was skin

or its silence.
    A light,
darkened, you could

touch. Yesterday
    I had to phone her,
my lover, calm

*

as I could, & say above
    the static that my father
was gone, but not quite—

first I must give
    his body,
breathed for, away. (25)

Hello, this is Sarah
    We harvested
your dad's liver

*

which tested fine
    This morning it went
to a 26-year-old

who needed it
    One kidney went locally
It was a match

The other I'll know
    tomorrow.
Do you authorize

                    *

the skin
    yes
the lungs

yes the heart *yes*
        the epidermis *yes*
the bone *no*

the small
        intestine *no*
the cornea *yes*—

                    *

(26)   Seeing her at last,
                  flown here, my wife-
              to-be—we held

          few words, only
                  each other.
          Desire's murmur

          is not fire
                  but water waded
          out into, or washed

                    *

over us, undertow
        we feed & are
fed from—

the absolution
        of skin.
We mourn,

moaning, making
        no one yet,
making nothing—

                *

our clothes husks
        shucked onto the cold
tile floor. Even nothing

a relief in that
        darkened room, no need
to speak. I held again   (27)

the speckled shells
        of her breasts & heard
there the ocean

                *

against my ear. For the first
        time, after,
I slept something

resembling sleep—
        quieted, quelled.
What we sought

in that afternoon dark
   was not the past, nor
a future I could no longer

                    *

picture—waking to find
   the pillow bowed
where her head once set—

but the ever
   present, a gift
made of it—

fleeting,
   then unmade
like our brief,

                    *

borrowed, narrow bed.

Rosetta

Alphabet of night.

The grammar of grief
    gets written each day

& lost—learnt again
    by stone, by small

sliver, hieroglyph.

    Morning
stays dark too long.

      The light takes
its own sweet

    time to arrive.
You, gone

into the afterlife
    of hollow hands,

faded photographs.

Night's black letters
    that require a song

to remember.

Charity

So many socks.

After the pair
the undertaker asks for
(I picture them black

beneath the fold
in your open casket,
your toes still cold)

what else to do.
Body bags
of old suits, shirts

still pressed, long
johns, the unworn,
unwashed wreckage

of your closet, too many
coats to keep, though I will save
so many. How can I

give away the last
of your scent? And still,
father, you have errands,

errant dry cleaning to pick up—
yellow tags whose ghostly
carbon tells a story

where to look. One
place closed
for good, the tag old.

One place with none
of your clothes,
just stares as if no one

ever dies, as if you
are naked somewhere,
& I suppose you are.

Nothing here.
The last place knows exactly
what I mean, brings me shirts

hanging like a head.
Starched collars
your beard had worn.

One man saying sorry, older lady
in the back saying how funny
you were, how you joked

with her weekly. *Sorry*—
& a fellow black man hands
your clothes back for free,

don't worry. I've learned death
has few kindnesses left.
Such is charity—so rare

& so rarely free—
that on the way back
to your emptying house

I weep. Then drive
everything, swaying,
straight to Goodwill—

open late—to live on
another body
& day.

Exit Music

In Baton Rouge bridges
end in midair, arms reaching
for the other shore

The lights & reek
of the cracker factory, refineries
seeping into the dark

I drive Cancer Alley
to the highwayside
where you will be buried

*

The smoke here is silver—

issuing like ash
or vespers over
the dirty river—

The night almost blue   (33)

*

I try & repair
what isn't there

*

When I leave your birth
place—now resting—

you are still
flowered & above ground

The earth soft
as flesh

The vault required
by the state

the grave would give way without

*

May you see
again

May I bless the man
who shot you

May I hold you
as he must have

praying & cursing
on your land covered by blood

(34)

His long mile to the nearest
house for help

Your swift flight
up & almost
alone, over

red fields I now own

*

Watch stopped like your heart
that they didn't want

*

Let the river run over

licking bones clean
like the vulture

The grey of the grave
swept away

The mangled moon
above the field

The dark don't stay
dark these days

Flag Day

O how I want
to waste my heart
on things that don't

matter much—
you dead two months,
about, & still

the light shining off
your bald head.
How I wish I could leave

or forget all my dead.
This morning, after nights
so hot I couldn't

quite sleep, rose up
to rain & a steady cool
like a tomb—

(36)   tonight the sky
swimming above
a trout, blue-grey

and shimmery,
we once caught. Cut
open, the pink

fish-flesh of the sunset.
To waste all I want—
to know no more

of midnight, of ordering
stones & choosing plots,
of giving all

your insides away.
See them spread
like the innards of your house

up for auction across
your browning yard—
To waste

this heart once more
& have you
here, not silent, only

quiet, as before.

Asylum

Even the dead have their day.
Even the dead know sanctuary—

I sat myself down beneath a tree
like a cathedral ceiling, asking

the leaves to tide over me.

Lift up & walk the place, let
the rocks fill your shoes.

Nearby, the steady
sound of a rake, a giant

hand gathering
what once was green.

Who can wait

till winter, its white
straitjacket, hugging

us together tight.

*

(THE BOOK OF FORGETTING)

Nothing
can warm us,

or warn—

Hurry Up & Wait

Flying west, what's below—

square acres
dusted by white powder,

few reservoirs, trees
born bare—

the way you were—
we all—seasons

I have spent dodging
the wind, looking for it—

its heat all the way
from the coast—

or the cold—which rode you
to the Midwest, your next-

to-last home.   (43)

Years I lived here, on the plains,
rigging my sails

for the sea. Now you're gone
for good, it helps

knowing you
breathed this air, winded

or full—in it
the airplane touches

down light
as the snow that surrounds us.

Alongside the road,
driving home, like you

are now—something rare
in the skeletal trees—

two hawks, together, lean.

Wintering

I am no longer ashamed
how for weeks, after, I wanted
to be dead—not to die,

mind you, or do
myself in—but to be there
already, walking amongst

all those I'd lost, to join
the throng singing,
if that's what there is—

or the nothing, the gnawing—
So be it. I wished
to be warm—& worn—

like the quilt my grandmother
must have made, one side
a patchwork of color—

blues, green like the underside
of a leaf—the other
an old pattern of the dolls

of the world, never cut out
but sewn whole—if the world
were Scotsmen & sailors

in traditional uniforms.
Mourning, I've learned, is just
a moment, many,

grief the long betrothal
beyond. Grief what
we wed, ringing us—

(45)

heirloom brought
from my father's hot house—
the quilt heavy tonight

at the foot of my marriage bed,
its weight months of needling
& thread. Each straightish,

pale, uneven stitch
like the white hairs I earned
all that hollowed year—pull one

& ten more will come,
wearing white, to its funeral—
each a mourner, a winter,

gathering ash at my temple.

Snow in April

Winter, you are
the worst kind

of lover—soon
as I hope for good

you're gone
you return—cold

in hand—
bringing no flowers

(47)

Easter

is the last we spoke.
　　　We were light, & even joked
how many turkeys—*tons*—

flooded wild his farm.
　　　A week later he was dead
hunting them with a friend.

No more sneezes, or silence, or cornbread—
　　　no more wildness anywhere
it would seem. Only

the hector of him gone
　　　waking me, early, or uneasy
sent asleep. I dreamt

last night his lawn guy brought
　　　back the mower bought
off me for a song. Now, among

the adorations & sarcophagi
　　　in the museum—cool marble
that also shades

my daddy's head—I am awed
　　　& angry all over again,
in love with beauty, the tomb

doors whose figures, etched,
　　　outlast their dead.
For weeks

I waited. For weeks dumb hope
　　　to have him visit—
not in waking, though that

I'd kill for—
  settle instead
for his returning with my eyes

closed, his sewn again open.
  Nobody came. Love
is strange & almost

always too late—his stubborn
  grace I miss.
For once that Easter

I told him.
  Luck
is one word for it.

Dream the Day After Easter

He said being dead was a little
like living, only longer.

Spring Training

Like grass in rain,
my dead grow

at an amazing rate.

Meet me,
won't you, I've managed

to lose the key.

Death, you've outdone
yourself.

The lawn a little lake.

Pity

The cookies his neighbors brought by
     didn't taste like pity—

at my father's house
     for the first time, after, the locks

broken into, now new, when cross
     the street *comes*

a neighbor, cookies shrouded
     in tinfoil, a plate

I need not return.
     How long had the pair

kept vigil out the window
     for someone to set foot here

so they might make their offering?
     Had they begun baking

soon as they heard, knowing
     full well the dead

& those closest to them
     grow hungry?

Like bread
     the body rising.

Inside, his house filled
     with what killed him—

a dozen turkey decoys deflating,
     bright empty shells.

Another kind soul had taped a tarp
    over his open sunroof top.

Disarray, the rest. Who knows
    what goes where? After

all, it is dirt we return to—or fire
    we devour—the pool

we once swam out back
    now drained, flooding the street

in mock calamity—no longer
    the filter sucking

its lower lip & teeth
    like a child trying

hard not to weep.

Remains

These things the waves want,
thieves—kiss

the coursing sand, lick
the coarse shore smooth

as stone. Shells
that held

what no longer
lingers—orange peels

& the sun in shards.
The salt-dark

rising up
out of the surf

for us. The footprints
of weary seagulls

shorthand on the sand.

*

That thought the dirt don't want,
gifts—them sing

the drying mud, rock
the smooth barrows rough

as rock, apples
that fall

postponed, then disappear—
apple cores

& the shade filling up.
The light tumbling

down to the ground
above you. The gloves

of shiny statues
sing in the leaves.

(55)

*

Sing in the leaves
of shiny statues

for you. The gloves
down into the ground

the light tumbling
the shade filling up.

Apple cores, where
they disappear, now fall

as rock—apples, hornets,
the smooth barrows rough—

the drying mud, rock,
the gift—them sing

that thought the dirt don't want.

Codicil

May God or whoever else
    spare you

the arms of bereavement
    specialists—

grant mercy from the Team
    dedicated to your transition

in this difficult time
    yet who won't tell you

a thing & know far less.
    Those innocent, interminable,

polite, unreachable
    voices over the phone—

do not suffer those—
    they are unlike death

who does not ask
    or give one whit

for your death certificate
    they need

duplicates of.
    No, originals.

No, now three letters
    of testamentary

six pounds of flesh—
    whatever's left.

(57)

Hell is not a live
        voice—just listen

to the complete menu
        as our options have changed.

Press One
        for Purgatory.

Two for shame.
        Three to get ready

Four for blame.
        Five years

of phone calls to sort
        your death out—

& one day, the avenging angel
        of telemarketing leaves

a message not asking
        after you, but acting

as if you & she
        had spoken, today—

*Paul, just wanted
        to get back to you*

about the cruise.

My response
        was what the afterlife

must be like—
    quick, mean, a piece

of my mind & passing
    along no peace—

just righteousness—if ever
    she called back

I said, *I'd kill her*—
    & not with kindness

as does the phone.
    Better to go it alone.

Memorial Day

Thunder knocks
loud on all the doors.

Lightning lets you
inside every house,
white flooding

the spare, spotless rooms.
Flags at half mast.

And like choirboys,
clockwork, the dogs
ladder their voices

to the dark, echoing off
each half-hid star.

Grief

The borrowed handkerchief
where she wept

returned to me months later,
starched, pressed.

Father's Day

Outside St. Cloud
        I begin to think
of my father, dead

over a year—
        his grave
no stone

makes sense for.
        Even the shortest grasses
now are taller

than he is.
        Gone are the days
you could, in flight,

without radar, find your way
        using water towers
of towns that

few maps name.
        A flag flaps
in the wind, or the wind

winches Old Glory, hard
        to tell.
The blood of a bent deer

darkens the road.
        What else—
you would love

the lake as much as the boat
        being drug, engine up,
its back stenciled: FISH PIMP.

At the Freedom Mart
       sitting patient, upright
in the driver's seat,

windows down, smokes
       on the dash,
a bearded dog waits

in a buzzcut
       welcoming summer, looks
as if he could just start

the car & steer us home.

Elegy

The cemetery bench
still warm.

Harvest

There's a moon with your name
& it wanes. Casts shadows giant

& low, like the bones
borrowed from your body—

broken machine
who breathes—

an anemone, many-
limbed & speechless.

We plant you inside
another body as if the earth,

which swallows you slow.
Today the last

of the fields you own
will be sold, unseen—

(65)

ground that grows
up around you, the brine

of the brain. The land survey
arrives late—a skeleton

seen after the flesh it fits
has gone. The moon

cold in hand & heavy,
a coin holding

your eyes closed. Come
see here what washes

ashore: the spare
cursive of your stray hair.

Anniversary

The day will come

when you'll be dead longer
than alive—thankfully

not soon.
There are of course years

long before, without you
breathing—and your years

without me even
an idea. Then there are those

infant months, when I knew
your voice, your bearded

face, not your name—
at least to speak

it aloud. And in the night,   (67)
father, I cried out

and in the day—
like now.

*

(CONFIRMATION)

A father's love
isn't milk, but blood—

Miscarriage

One week after, we make

love, again, for the first
time, hopeful

you're healed.
And the wind

still loud
against new windows—

the day dances
around us into

dark.
What remains

besides pain?
How to mourn what's just

a growing want?   (73)
The baby books

put away, the hand-me-downs

we'll never hand.
The heat shudders on

and against your chest
I nod

off, hearing your lone
heart whisper:

uh-huh, uh-huh, uh-
huh, uh-huh.

*

Expecting

Grave, my wife lies back, hands cross
her chest, while the doctor searches early
for your heartbeat, peach pit, unripe

plum—pulls out the world's worst
boombox, a Mr. Microphone, to broadcast
your mother's lifting belly.

The whoosh and bellows of mama's body
and beneath it: nothing. Beneath
the slow stutter of her heart: nothing.

The doctor trying again to find you, fragile
fern, snowflake. Nothing.
After, my wife will say, in fear,

impatient, she went beyond her body,
this tiny room, into the ether—
for now, we spelunk for you one last time

lost canary, miner of coal
and chalk, lungs not yet black—
I hold my wife's feet to keep her here—

and me—trying not to dive starboard
to seek you in the dark water. And there
it is: faint, an echo, faster and farther

away than mother's, all beat box
and fuzzy feedback. You are like hearing
hip-hop for the first time—power

hijacked from a lamppost—all promise.
You couldn't sound better, break-
dancer, my favorite song bumping

from a passing car. You've snuck
into the club underage and stayed!
Only later, much, will your mother

begin to believe your drumming
in the distance—our Kansas City
and Congo Square, this jazz band

vamping on inside her.

Starting to Show

She sleeps on the side
her heart is on—

sleeps facing the sun
that juts through our window

earlier and earlier. In the belly
of the sky the sun kicks

and cries. My wife
has begun to wear the huge

clothes of inmates, smuggling you
inside her—son

or daughter. I bring her
crackers and water.

Wardens of each other,
in the precincts

of unsteady sleep, we drift
off curled

like you are, listening
to the night breathe.

(77)

Ultrasound

The silent
movie of your spine.

We sit
in this darkened

room, waiting
for you to finish

your fits and starts
so we can see

your face. The ultrasound
a spotlight

you swim in,
bow. Your first

appearance is black
and white, like the beginning

of words, or a world. This
absurdist Dada happening,

your grainy newsreel
footage, heart-silhouette,

telling us what we may
want to know—

It's a boy.
Surrealist, shadow

boxer, you raise a hand
to shield your face

from our prying stares—
or to thumb

your way outta here.

First Kick

More like
a flicker, a far-
   off flutter

  beneath my
broad hand—
   then, two

weeks later,
   a nudge, a knee
as you elbow

round inside—
   acrobat, apple
of our eye

  we can't
yet see. You seed
  my mind

   with nicknames,
Buddy. Junior,
  you drift

like an astronaut
   tethered silver
to the mothership.

You are even better
  than fruit
floating in Jell-O!

  We cannot wait
to welcome you
   with ticker tape—

no slap—
when at last you arrive
and find life

on our puny planet.

Linea Nigra

Son, what we learn
your first trip
to Paris is this: you love
Indian cuisine, croissant,
and Fra Angelico—or maybe
that's me. Soon
as curry creeps mama's
lips you start to kick.
And kick. My hand
on her stomach's music
can send you to sleep—
though sometimes the ripeness
of mama's belly becomes
my bed, and inside
that melon you thump back.
Between your mother and me
it seems we are only one soul
sleeping—one of us awake
while the train cradles
the other into dreams.
Will one day you remember
all the places your father
brought you, like I do
mine? The words for *mountain*
and *mine* can sound the same
in a Frenchman's mouth—
mine can get us a meal, not
much more. In stores I point
and shoot, like our cameras
that capture what our eyes
cannot quite. Son, come soon,
not too soon, and we'll swaddle you tight

like the black man outside
the Gare d'Austerlitz sleeping
in a golden solar blanket
bright and brittle as a bride's
thrown bouquet.

Montagne Noire

Not quite *custard*
or *mustard*—the name
of that green stuff
inside a lobster's head
escapes me. Crustacean,
amphibian, son—you float
in your own sauces
like mandarin oranges.
Duck confit. Pâté
de foie gras. Every day
with the Black
Mountain crouched outside
our window, we eat
till we cannot remember
hunger, then down wine
till we forget. You sit
like something on the tip
of my tongue—a word
hard enough to find, much less
in French—you are a euphemism,
dauphin, whose name
we can't wait to know.
How many words
are there for stone?
What language do you
dream in, garçon? Not
ours yet, not *delicieux*—
though you're that too—
not *roe,* nor *meringue*—
not till we've flown home
do I recall the name for that
mossy glowing green
where a lobster's brain
should be: *tamale.*

(84)

Gravida

You are the inside
of a clock, workings,

its steady tock
your grandfather never

will get to see—
You weave veins

on mama's stomach
like riverways

or back roads on maps
that no longer fold—

You spin like a world—
the weight of it

my wife carries
swelling her

feet like streams
after storm

or rain into the sea

(85)

Quickening

Fourth of July
Sag Harbor, Long Island

On the beach the fireworks bloom
    above us, their boom
and brightness, and my goddaughter

slips asleep. These days
    inside mama you don't so much
kick as wrestle, an elbow

then your butt budding
    out her belly. We lie
by the water and watch the dark

lap the sand and scrub-filled shore.
    Another ultrasound shows
you are my son, alright—head down

like a monk, burrowing, your profile
    and pout only I seem to see.
When will you arrive to usher us

into your arms? It is we
    who will be born,
not you. After the fanfare

for the country's birth—the smoke
    and strong gunpowder smell
to remind us what once was there—

we'll walk back home
    across the dark,
unalone.

(86)

Lightening

The body is a strange place
to be. Like belief,

you live in mama's belly
and we can't wait to see you

breathe. Till then, your mother's
sleepless and wakes before

the light lists into the room.
I wish sleep to summon

her, to rock her
like you do with your judo

and kung fu. Scuba diver, Sub-
mariner, you're adrift

in a ship propelled
by butterfly kicks. Or

(87)

you're Popsicle after
Popsicle—grape and red

staining mother's tongue
like your name we are

telling no one. Boy
in a bubble, the body

is where you live
for now—practicing

the twist, the two-
step, you tango till dawn

soon as mama
lies down—in twilight

sometimes you jab just
at me, your mother still,

and at last, asleep.
Can I miss you long

before you're born? I see
you now as lost

at sea, mother's stomach a sail
tugging you ashore—

my hands on the rigging—
how you turn, even now,

toward my voice.

(88)

Nesting

The heart isn't even
human. Prehistoric,

painful, in the chest it chooses
to beat itself silly.

A bundle of bees
in a hive breathing.

Without warning,
the story it tells

to no one ends—
or begins, a shadow

grown beneath the breast.
Fights

and does not fit. Tonight
I'll broom what

(89)

soon will be your nursery,
easing the spiders out

into relentless rain—
shooing bees

that gather like honey
against the screens.

The machines
that trace our breathing

in hospitals lie—
the heart is no line

crossing the palm,
no jagged green—

just this twin
fist opening.

Labor Day

It's knotted in the ninth
after a double sends Manny
home for the Sox.
Still the season seems lost—

you're into
extra innings too—
days overdue—
stranded on base

like machinery
on the moon. Are bodies
where we're born? You've grown
under my skin—

not just mama's,
where we watch you
stretch and poke
her ribs, practice

jujitsu. We joke   (91)
about you and hope
you're soon. We wait
and prepare over

and over, sweep
what's already clean.
On Labor Day, we're sent
to the hospital to see

if they can induce
mom and you—to deduce
or tease you out into air—
are sent home packing

to be born tomorrow.
Why would you
bother coming here?
Your godfather

says you just don't know
all the candy
that awaits, the ballgames
and summer's long sway.

With his lobster
legs the catcher crouches
as if in labor, his fingers
giving signals

like a newborn reaching out
toward the light. Full count.
The season's far too short—and not
short at all—soon enough

you'll be kicking, meeting
us whom you only know
by voice, a blind date made
over the phone. You're late.

Stood up, we head home
in a daze to attempt
sleep, watch the game
and pray in the eleventh

Big Papi knocks one
out the park—
all night your foot
juts just under

your mother's heart.

Breaking Water

The earth has no edge
    except this: waiting

for you to get born
    but quick. Your galaxy

inside mama keeps on
    expanding, her stomach

a planetarium, solar
    system of one. Son,

anything pressed
    against mama's skin

leaves saturnine rings.
    Her belts go begging—

and her wedding rings.

While scientists try to decide
    whether Pluto's still

a planet, you rotate
    on your axis, play

Asteroids with mama's pelvis.
    I now know pain

is part of any journey—
    that this is the opposite

of grief, but grief
    the only way I know

to describe waiting
      and waiting without

knowing, hoping one day
      joy will arrive.

Or return. You must cross
      breaking waves

of pain, the canal
      of your birth, mama's

breathing and me barely—and none
      too soon you're here

named for your grandfather,
      squalling.

Nativity

I believe birth a lengthy process
    meant to help us believe
    in the impossible.

I believe the body knows
    more than we do.

I believe pregnancy is meant
    to teach us patience,
    then impatience. To ready
    for what cannot be.

I believe it does not matter
    what I believe.

I believe aches now,
    heartbreak later.

I believe the body is meant
    to emerge from another body,
    to merge with it.

I believe that the body begins
    far outside the skin.

I believe in you mewling my name
    until it is yours,
    then mine again.

I believe that heat can stay
    with us for days,
    that cold is only an instant,
    then always.

Crowning

Now that knowing means nothing,
now that you are more born
than being, more awake
than awaited, since I've seen
your hair deep inside mother,
a glimpse, grass in late
winter, early spring, watching
your mother's pursed, throbbing,
purpled power, her pushing
you for one whole hour, two,
almost three, almost out,
maybe never, animal smell
and peat, breath and sweat
and mulch-matter, and at once
you descend, or drive, are driven
by mother's body, by her will
and brilliance, by bowel,
by wanting and your hair
peering as if it could see, and I saw
you storming forth,
taproot, your cap of hair half
in, half out, and *wait, hold
it there,* the doctors say, and
she squeezing my hand, her face
full of fire, then groaning your face
out like a flower, blood-bloom,
crocused into air, shoulders
and the long cord still rooting
you to each other, to the other
world, into this afterlife
among us living, the cord
I cut like an iris, pulsing,
then you wet against mother's chest

still purple, not blue, not yet
red, no cry,
warming now, now opening
your eyes midnight
blue in the blue black dawn.

Colostrum

We are not born
with tears. Your

first dozen cries
are dry.

It takes some time
for the world to arrive

and salt the eyes.

Jaundice

It's hard being
human. This morning yellow

overtook you, a thousand
yolks broken beneath

your skin. Splotches
of red, and you not rousing,

drowsy, listless—your head dips
like a drunk's, or a duck

in a shooting gallery. Wrung,
we ring and bring you to a doctor

whose worried brown face
I try hiding from your mother—

she weeps over your body
mottled, bare, losing weight—

(99)

your black, burnt-
looking belly button, even

your feet flushed.
What color

should you be?
Hard to say

my black-eyed
susan, barely born, the flowers

brought by you
and last week's visitors

freshly cut, bowed in water.
Tomorrow maybe

we'll breathe.
For now we worry

the waiting room, watch
the clock wind us—

television showing the anniversary
of September's calamities

that seem worlds away
and yesterday.

You roll to the nursery
to tan under blue light

we pray will bake
the poison out. In fever

your body burns
like a martyr. Pietà,

hothouse hope, you rise up
hours later—lighter

and darker too. The yellow
leaving you. Eyes

still not white
but opening slow. What color

should you be?
After mama nurses

you, I feed you formula
on doctor's orders, color

of buttermilk, eggnog
maybe—saying

wake up, the almost
milk everywhere spilling.

Rooting

On our evening walks
my newborn and I don't much talk—

he can't yet—though
in the dark that grows

around us like a want,
we walk—and I swat

away gnats, poisoned mosquitoes,
the world's deepest noise

my son barely notices.
What is it

he can see? The city
thundering him to sleep.

Arm raised as if voting
or volunteering.

At home, my teenager's
sudden lightning—

overnight she's grown,
holds herself. Comports.

The gnats, and the night—
the stroller's swift roll—

then something unknown
tosses him awake

weeping like a widow.

Nothing will calm
him but my arms.

A father's love
isn't milk, but blood—

is not wine,
nor words nor even wise

but groceries, the light
bill paid on time—

is not two o'clock
feeds—necessarily—but rocking

a son to sleep,
making sure the wife

and children eat.
How can you convince

anyone else to sleep?
Thankless, it is

like my dead
father's silence, in which I read

and must, only love—
words rarely heard, forget

touch—but now
know without

hearing, the way I know his beard
in the grave keeps growing.

Beasting

Like the rest of us
You swim

In your own piss.

*

Where does the body
begin? Is it when

you emerged with the sun
on the horizon, purple

as dawn—or when
you quit breathing

blood, the cord I cut
while you still slept

or so it seemed.
You finally

holler
you're here.

*

Sleep
For Sale

*

Wolf boy
dawn-born

Thick dark
hair everywhere

                *

Cased in wax
Mummified

By vernix, that white
Which wrapped you

Umpteen weeks
Let you live

Like a pharaoh
Prepared

For the next world
Now

Mostly gone   (105)

                *

Some say the first
taste of breast

holds traces of blood—
it is the wildness

within us, the wolf
we nurse with—

and this
is called *beasting*.

*

Baby for rent
Or lease

Option to own
Cheap

*

Your body is what
I can barely believe—

your fingers small, stuck
in a sleeve, knotted

in my hair, and yours
slowly leaves.

Autumn's twin,
you welcome winter

and the wolf moon
baying above our house

soon enough haunted
by your toys & bright voice.

For now, the baby monitor's
soft static, where

all night we overhear
you, lowing.

*

Like a saint's, your body
is no longer your own—

you with your mother's feet,
daddy's nose—

*

back of your head a halo
of bones

that haven't yet
closed.

Teething

Son, the words that aren't
yet yours
are the ones we want

most to hear. Forget
the dead, the executions
and the moon that disappears

like most everything, see
how it returns?
Forget those lists

of the lost that appear
like paperwhites
at year's end, narcissuses,

something to aspire to—
so many forgot
or not

even mentioned. Forget
the assassins, the foolish
critics, the silence

we all learn. The cold
that's going around.
The ghosts

of the words
that go away. Instead,
keep trying

your tongue like a flame
about to start, the sound
of flint striking stone, your mouth.

Teething

The mouth is the most
potent instrument an infant
possesses—no wonder

you put your tongue
to anything, or anything
in your mouth. Roots

of teeth teasing just below
your gums. Drool
is your muse,

your song or cry
always rising. Unlike us,
you love being

changed. It is only
sleep you mind—missing
the world's noise, what wisdom

the widows know. The bell
of your mouth ringing
in morning.

(109)

Teething

Mote of days—

We carry you
strapped to our bellies

like a bomb.
Head against

our hearts, a hand
during an anthem, you sleep

still, quiver
then quiet.

We are all
within a veil.

Soon the small, starting
sounds—you slur

what will be words,
aren't quite—

tomorrow's missteps

we already miss—
ten-teen, or *fool*

instead of *school.*
Soon enough sentences—

your old words savored
and mourned, like your first

shorn hair.

Teething

When will we be tired?

I really love my neck.
I keep care of it.

I take care of it
& keep care of it.

They sound the same.

When I was a baby
I had zero teeth!

That means none.

I wish I had a mailbox
at my house.

Because there are
mailboxes there:

Three.

(111)

Greening

It never ends, the bruise
     of being—messy,
untimely, the breath

of newborns uneven, half
     pant, as they find
their rhythm, inexact

as vengeance. Son,
     while you sleep
we watch you like a kettle

learning to whistle.
     Awake, older,
you fumble now

in the most graceful
     way—grateful
to have seen you, on your own

     steam, simply eating, slow,
     chewing—this bloom
of being. Almost beautiful

how you flounder, mouth full, bite
     the edges of this world
that doesn't want

a thing but to keep turning
     with, or without you—
with. With. Child, hold fast

I say, to this greening thing
     as it erodes
and spins.

Thirst

What blossoms
    is loss—
last year's ash

fills a tin from the grill
    that fed us all
last summer like a father—

that black belly
    rusty, its grate
you scrape, hopefully not too clean—

the past where
    taste lives,
seasoning—sudden weeds

taller than even
    you dreamed, bending
bare arms to the earth

to yank them out by their hair.   (113)
    The hollies finally
given up on—

the dead harder
    to root out than
you'd think, worms

weaving round the dirt
    black, lush, clinging—
the ferns somehow returned,

planted in that heat wave
    last summer, remember, sweat
stinging the eyes, wilting—

now their green
    palms wide open
in offering. The steady

consolation of things
    returning—lilac
and dogwood, sweet woodruff, even

the stones shine
    in the sun. White blooms
soon gone—

soothing thud
    of the neighbor girl playing
catch, catgut kissing leather

or missed, the ball landing soft
    in our yard's
deep grass—*so sorry*

for your loss—only the tulips
    refusing to rise
this spring, stung

by the freezer all winter
    we kept them in.
Like any good son, mine

still tends the dirt, watering
    the bulbs long after
they're done—with his little cup

tries to fill the darkness up.

*

Blessings

for my stepdaughter

May you never see
the diseased carp
being carried from the lake
like a lost girl, limp.

May the white dog
of Mercy drag you
from the car long before
it pours into flame.

May Mercy come
when called.

May you never lose
the family dog through
early ice, as your father did,

then weeks later spot
him below, frozen, eyeing you
skating just

out of reach, looking
like heaven to him.

May you exceed
our expectations, not
our reach, our reach
but not our grasp,

our homes
not our arms.

*

(THE BOOK OF THE BODY)

My words are glass
made clear

by breath
and hands—

Pietà

I hunted heaven
for him.

No dice.

Too uppity,
it was. Not enough

music, or dark dirt.

I begged the earth empty
of him. Death

believes in us whether
we believe

or not. For a long while
I watch the sound

of a boy bouncing a ball
down the block

take its time
to reach me. Father,

find me when
you want. I'll wait.

(121)

Truce

*Tell me
about the body.*

It's empty.

*No, tell me
about the body.*

It can be donated
or burnt.

Burnt it is—

Or buried.

Or believed in.

Where's the soul?
Hidden.

Where.
Everywhere.

And the breath.
Only wind.

And after—

Sun and
snow both.

Stigmata

Rain, and the reasons.

Heaven is your hair
mostly gone.

I beg of you—

the winter
with its hands

bare, the branches—

arrive early
into our arms.

Limbo

Empty your arms of all
they own.

Now, bring me
what remains—

like a saint's
scattered bones

or stories told
in glass, stained.

Ruth

Every pore mourns.
Not the brain, nor
the chest where bereavement

nests, but the body, whole—
how it burns.
The ache of new bone

being grown.

*

That summer the faith
of a fever bent me
to my knees. Or flat

on my aching back, shivering
like a tree. I cannot keep anything
down all week. I thrush

& thrash, quarantined, thirst   (125)
to know what's happening
among the rooms

of the living.

*

Bedridden, I can barely see
the clear, glacial lake
where tiger mussels swept upstream

by boat & accident
cut the feet, devouring
everything, like grief,

till there's no more—
which, next year, is what
they'll be—like my father

is already.

*

Sharper than stone
or woe, the mussels soon
will eat themselves

into extinction—
two summers
later, floating far

from the shore—
you cannot mourn
forever—my infant son will cry

with delight while passed,
kicking, between our
watery hands. For now,

the ashen world without him

*

has come to live,
unspoken, a sore
along my tongue—

swollen like an adder
whose prey takes weeks
to devour. My skin

on fire, wished
to be shed—or molting,
swallowing stone.

My soon hollow bones.

*

They shine in me a light.
I lie still,
transported into the white

hum, naked beneath
a shroud, while they sift
& read my blood.

It's mum. No one
can name
what's sought

to undo me this season—
some bug, locust god,
or hex? The dead

crouched on my chest.

*

Autumn now all
around us, the abscess
slow erodes—

of life there's always
only less.
Even healing

hurts. Our bodies
leave us little
choice—scars

that way are ruthless—
what's mended
stitched stronger

that what gaped

*

there before. So this
is what
it means to mourn:

the horse pills
I choke back
for weeks—like the food

you must down them with—
are almost more
painful than whatever

they cure.

*

Lips cracked open
like an egg, half-dead,
all night I toss & churn—

featherless bird
its mother feeds
from her own mouth—

maw of what sustains
that almost
swallows

us whole—
the pain newborn
& ravenous, fledgling,

then flown.

The Book of the Body

There is the body inside
the body—the one

not of skin but
sinew—soul.

Brother of mine,
ingrown twin.

Belief lives
in the bone—

is what has broken
inside me,

not heart. You can live
without that

I've learned—
I know now

you can be buried
without one stitch

of what was once inside.
Forget even

the body—that
is the only way

to learn to live
as one. Let me be

like the child who knows
& loves her youthful belly,

says she'll miss it
when soon, her bones grown,

it melts overnight away.

Annunciation

Fra Angelico
Convento di San Marco, north corridor

Do not believe

angels are easy.
Instead, terrible,

terrific
in the oldest sense—

the ground giving

way beneath
your feet.

Is the phone
saying, *There's nothing*

left to do,
kiddo.

Or knocking to say,
You must do

as I tell you—giving
birth to virgin pain

no pleasure before.

Their words blue
& burning, like a flue.

Their every wing
a tongue.

Annunciation

Fra Angelico
Convento di San Marco, Cell 3

Do not answer
angels. Or ask.

Simply allow
them in as if you meant

to invite them. As if the sun.
The moon blue

as an angel's wing, every
feather a peacock eye

every eye winking.
Lower

your head. This swimming
sight. Through

your one window   (133)
the light limps. Through

the night you kneel. Bent
in pain or is it

birth—what you must
understand is that

the herald & the horror
are the same.

He's dead. You're
late. The world

retreats, the words
spill, stay permanent

in the air. Over the years
you earn here

not a larger cell
but one smaller

& smaller.

(134)

Stillborn

You are not still,
nor born,
now never

will be. *It doesn't
look good,* says
the attending—

the ultrasound fuzzy
as a grave rubbing.
Your insides

*

are out. We peer
into your head
while I try seeing

into our doctor's—
never met before—
his eyes silent in the glow

of what won't. Your heart
all fluid, mine
no stone, only a sliver—

*

no pictures
to keep, just my wife
keening & me

& my eye's
pinhole camera burning
beneath the eclipse

of you. Father
of forgetting—before
you're even here,

*

or forsaken, we must
send our regrets, addressing
you whose many names,

my word, we'll never
know. You a ship
unchristened

in the harbor
of her—anchored,
on fire.

Arbor Day

It's supposed to be beautiful tomorrow
should be New England's motto.

Instead it's Shut up & drive.
Or, I never met a lane
I didn't like. Often two at the same time.

Once I watched, while the rest
of us pulled over, someone drive past
then turn left—crash—

into a flashing ambulance.
At least she used
her turn signal.

So when we lost the wanted, not-
yet child, it was supposed to be
nice outside

but wasn't. Inside the baby
we already had cried
to be read to—

(137)

my wife listing room to room.
In brisk, unbloomed April
only the crocus have pulled through.

Tomorrow yard waste
pickup resumes, my helpful
neighbor reminds me—I recollect

last fall's late leaves in sacks
mostly torn behind the house
where all winter they sat,

half preserved, half rot.
Our lawn mostly mud, I lug
the damp, heavy bags—

unwieldy as a body given
six months of winter,
or more—& of course,

or luckily, only
one split. The black
leaves spilling their ink

across the still-brown lawn.
By glove & shovel I shove
the loam into another bag—

IDEAL FOR COMPOSTING SELF—
which, on its own, weighted
along the curb, doesn't manage

to stand. The dead leaves
lean there for weeks,
fraying, a reminder of all

we get wrong, & fate—
turns out I was too early—
before men come at dawn one day

& whisk everything away.

City of God

Closed for renovations.

Closed for cleaning
till next September

Closed due to rain—

not the kind that clears
after hours of falling

but that keeps
the streets still

haunted by heat.

Rain that blooms you
awake again

in the city
everyone claims, no one

wants to pay for.

Please excuse
our dust.

The streets crowded
with tourists

in bright shirts
& matching drinks

begging for wings.

Memorial Day

I wake early to join
      the others dying
of sweat, or breath, trying

to return to the bodies
      we once owned—
slow going on a quick

track. We orbit
      the fake grass, sun
already high enough to burn

the eyes or arms, windmilling
      for all it's worth.
We keep finding ourselves

in each other's way—silent
      we spin, a cavalcade
of future pain. And then,

in the blue beside
      the ring, up springs
a proper parade—

traffic lined up & ashen
      veterans, three left,
bow their heads

while names are read—
      is that a prayer
I can't make out

above the quick trinity
      of rifle fire, smoke
clouding the air?

None flinch.
    We keep pace along
with our shortening shadows,

every ache a wish.

Sight

All sight is double—
I spot
among your leavings
this old X-ray,

peering into some part
of you I never knew
needed mending—an arm
or suspect heart.

Since you've gone,
my eye doctor
& father, I've never
seen another—

*

but today, grown hazy,
I finally pay
at the ophthalmologist
& wait like anyone—

no more a doctor's son.
Called in, orphaned,
I stare at the mirror
till it turns to letters

& I read aloud what's there.
ZVHRC—
the orderly will not
shake my hand, only

*

takes down my eyes
are dry. When finally
the doctor enters
the dilated dark,

she shines blue light
to stare behind my iris
while I tell her all
you once were—

or try. It is she
who leads
your life now
& doesn't even know

*

your name. In my past
tense she won't hear
you are dead, says instead
to tell you my vision

has grown just a hair
more shortsighted
since. The mirror holds letters,
not words. She bends

my heavy head to burn
my eyes with tears, blurred.

Miracle Removal

i.m. Helen Hill

This world is rigged
with ruin.

Rain,
and its remains.

In the yard drought
fills the empty jars—

houses on stilts
still lean.

Sweet as revenge, the grass
devours the abandoned

dream house, unfinished kitchen
where cows now graze.

What angels
I would wrestle.

(144)

Sorrow

The dogs ate what we did
    only days

later. Like angels
    they roam the countryside

belonging to no one.
    And everyone.

We feed them like sorrow
    to keep them at bay

& to make them stay.
    Like heaven we begin

to expect them each day—
    put out a cracked plate

just in case. Like the dead
    they are impossible

(145)

to tame.

Pilgrimage

Your love,
Two-headed cow
  —R.E.M.

We were west of it,
home I mean, and I was trying

near Death Valley
to write a poem called Heaven

and failing. Impossible,
Paradise—

which is why
we keep reaching.

Instead, the desert

we'd soon enter,
windows down, driving, the heat

(146) blowing us drier
than ever, shirt soaked through.

We'd stopped earlier to see
the sheep with two faces

who lived only an hour—

a six-legged steer
and the World's Largest

Prairie Dog. Which wasn't
ever alive, but worth the price.

It was almost autumn—

sturgeon moon
lifting above the mountains

and mesas—even its light
seemed full of heat.

Paradise was promise,
the poem thankfully lost.

All signs read: Here
was fought the battle

no one won.
Thinner then, I believed

in something moving beyond

the wind. What
did I know then

of extinction? It was all   (147)
I wrote about.

Envy the dead—
the flowers, their unmade beds.

How well they dress.

Here I was writing a poem
called Heaven

actually about the earth.
It shook beneath us.

Almost there, windmills
rose up

out of the desert,
churning, rowing

the very air
they made power

out of, and for—
an unseen that made them

move, and mean.

Lower Haight

1991

There are cars that carry quiet—
not here. Here the boys
BOOM-budda-buh-bum, buh-BOOM
as their cars roll, bop, & lean

down the street. No alarms,
no birds—salsa six a.m.
beneath your window
wakes you. *More bounce*

to the ounce. Words fly
from windows, spreading summer—
Thinking of a master plan
while your insides echo. Car windows

throb like the pulse
of a long-distance runner
or lover, still
jogging at the stoplight.

Aftershocks. Heads bob
like apples, choruses spill
out the wheeling world
into the one we walk

or sleep through, at least
till the tape gets rewound, starts
again. *Nee-EEEE-ah, Nee-EEEE-
ah*—the cars call to us, Richter

scale, ritual, rouse us
from dream, or speech—a second
heartbeat—rattling the rickety
cages of our ribs, our solitary.

(149)

Gravity

I have tried telling this before—
how the light stabbed its way
out of the clouds, rays
aimed everywhere—
no, it was the earth that day
drawing light out of the sky,
heavy, gravity pulling
the light to rest on its chest,
a ladder leaning—
in the valley north of the City
of Angels, mountains around us,
my passenger a twin, one
half of two, their mother
killed a year
or so before, helicopter
catching a power line—
gone—and I, knowing nothing
then, or too much, said
little, maybe *sorry*
which isn't all
you can say, but mostly—
though I didn't know that then—
and we were fighting
with my warbling tape deck,
no doubt, when we saw it—
tumbling, end
over end across the highway,
a car flipping and spitting up
dust and God knows
what else—midair—
and almost before I could reach
the shoulder, my friend out
across the lanes, racing
to the crumpled car,
to his mother—even then
I knew it was her he hoped

to meet—instead, in the scorched
grass of the median, a spare
or spared shoe, books flapping
their wings, and a man, dazed, somehow
thrown clear—
kneeling. We were not
the first, already some off-duty nurse
or Samaritan beside him, within
seconds, asking
what I should have—*are you*
alright? He held
no answers, no tongue
for where he had just
been, almost stayed, the car turtled
over on its back, its brokenness
that could be
our bodies, not yet
our lives—or his—and my friend
the twin almost there in time,
me slow behind, the last
of the first—scared to see—   (151)
looking on in horror
and wonder, clothes tossed
everywhere now no one would wear—
the broken mirrors missing
bodies they once
were conjoined to—
closer than they appear—
a blinding, splintered sky
helpless we soon would turn
and sail off under.

The Mission

Back there then I lived
      across the street from a home

for funerals—afternoons
      I'd look out the shades

& think of the graveyard
      behind Emily Dickinson's house—

how death was no
      concept, but soul

after soul she watched pour
      into the cold

New England ground.
      Maybe it was the sun

of the Mission,
      maybe just being

more young, but it was less
      disquiet than comfort

days the street filled with cars
      for a wake—

children played tag
      out front, while the bodies

snuck in the back. The only hint
      of death those clusters

of cars, lights low
      as talk, idling dark

as the secondhand suits
        that fathers, or sons

now orphans, had rescued
        out of closets, praying

they still fit. Most did. Most
        laughed despite

themselves, shook
        hands & grew hungry

out of habit, evening
        coming on, again—

the home's clock, broke
        like a bone, always

read three. Mornings or dead
        of night, I wondered

who slept there & wrote letters
        I later forgot

I sent my father, now find buoyed up
        among the untidy

tide of his belongings.
        He kept everything

but alive. I have come to know
        sorrow's

not noun
        but verb, something

that, unlike living,
    by doing right

you do less of. The sun
    is too bright.

Your eyes
    adjust, become

like the night. Hands
    covering the face—

its numbers dark
    & unmoving, unlike

the cars that fill & start
    to edge out, quiet

cortége, crawling, half dim, till
    I could not see to see—

*

(BOOK OF HOURS)

*Wake me when
we get there*

not a moment before.

The light here leaves you
lonely, fading

as does the dusk
that takes too long

to arrive. By morning
the mountain moving

a bit closer to the sun.

This valley belongs
to no one—

except birds who name
themselves by their songs

in the dawn.
What good

are wishes, if they aren't   (159)
used up?

The lamp of your arms.

The brightest
blue beneath the clouds—

We guess
at what's next

unlike the mountain

who knows it
in the bones, a music

too high
to scale.

*

The burnt,
blurred world

where does it end—

The wind
kicks up the scent

from the stables
where horseshoes hold

not just luck but
beyond. But

weight. But a body

that itself burns,
begs to run.

The gondola quits just
past the clouds.   (161)

The telephone poles
tall crosses in the road.

Let us go
each, into the valley—

turn ourselves
& our hairshirts

inside out, let the world
itch—for once—

Black like an eye

bruised night brightens
by morning, yellow

then grey—
a memory.

How the light was alive.

All day the heat a heavy,
colored coat.

I want to lie
down like the lamb—

down & down
till gone—

shorn of its wool.
(162)   The cool

of setting & rising
in this valley,

the canyon between us
shoulders our echoes.

Moan, & make way.

*

Leaving the valley—
the pines

overwhelm me.
Candles aimed

at the above.
How to fit—

the road's shadow
stark & lengthened.

Climbing was easier
than descent

which rushes us past
the blue

of Donner Pass.
Hard to believe

here, by the angelic lake,
stranded, the dead went

unburied & the living
went mad. Divvying

up the lost so no one
ate their kin.

Winter gets inside—

Better to die
than eat of your father,

body without blood?
The dust

along the parched road remembers—
wants only a spark

to send it all, every needle, up
in flame.

*

The sun's small fury
feeds me.

Wind dying down.

We delay, & dither,
then are lifted

into it, brightness
all about—

O setting.
O the music

as we soar
is small, yet sating.

What you want—

Nobody, or nothing
fills our short journeying.   (165)

Above even the birds,
winging heavenward,

the world is hard
to leave behind

or land against—
must end.

I mean to make it.

Turning slow beneath
our feet,

finding sun, seen
from above,

this world looks
like us—mostly

salt, dark water.

*

You could spend
a lifetime hoping

to mend the moon.

Tonight let's try—
bent to the fallen

needles, the pines, my hands
weaving

& wanting.

The half-moon
of your heart.

The stars are
so far.

Their light even
death does not end,   (167)

late arrives—

they bear
up the world

by their strings
& by example.

Shut your eyes.

The mantle
of midnight grown

light along my shoulder.
Each star a stone

in the river of sky—
the Milky Way's bright tide

wringing me awake.

*

Damn the dark.
Keep me company

till morning,
then leave me

with only the light!

Let night rain
its names over me.

I wish to wash
my face in the furnace—

September
too short—

& the days.

Think of me when
the moon stares   (169)

its skull above you—
summoning the shadow—

while the stars bleach
slowly the sky,

bluing.

The few fields
    forgive you—

give way to valleys
    inside the mind

that themselves fill
    with wildflowers—

brown-eyed susans
    swaying, saying

something to the bees
    about beginning

about being
    patient & what is

beyond all this—
    it is always the bloom,

(170)

that undoing,
    does me in.

The dogwood we planted
    for my son

now dying—

But it is not the autumn
    I mean to mention.

Nor the winter
    that has overcome

the air just today,
        11th November, & because

I can name it, the end,
        I will.

Still, the bent wood

of a chair, indoors, will
        hold you, the small green

leftover from summer
        will raise you up long

as it can, long
        as you don't fight it.

Being means believing,
        if only what we don't

know yet—   (171)
        this quiet, coming,

rare & rarer, but still
        there, below

the buzzing, just there,
        opened after

the white of winter's letters.

*

How to listen
to what's gone—

To moan & learn—

The geese don't
seem to mind

winter anymore—stay
put & graze.

No more their calls
against the dusk.

Nor their arrows
silhouetted against

this tintype sky—

its silver face, once
touched, begins

to fade fingerprint-grey.

Letters
I've never sent.

This life
we're only renting.

Battered the world is—
bartered—

wander over it,
the stars finding

us wanting.

*

The dark must live
in this valley, rising

each night to meet
the starved sky—mountains

where the light resides
& lingers long after

sun up & dies. I am
only human, the snow

seems to know—
chills my cracked hands

& takes hold my mouth
till all talk is fog—

out the clouded window
the snow sloughs

slow into the river, beyond
the old mill, the liquor store

selling warmth
& the chill after. The rocks

along the shore
bleached to bone, the water

like a wish rushing past—

Winter's thunder—

the snow butcher
paper wrapping the no-longer

of the lawn.
Ice, then

this echo haunting
the eaves.

I don't mind
dying—

it is the living—

Icicles asking
not if,

but when.

Carry me home.

And downtown,
on its own,

the tree breathes,
the awning—

a hive of startled
unseen starlings.

Does the wind wonder
   about us—

the way it blows
   the blossoms down

it must—the birds start
   their bargaining early

before we awaken

& do our own—
   which may

be too late.

The bare beach
   in winter.

Dogs in the distance,
   the frozen whitecaps.

How far could we walk

across that water?
   Gulls like vultures

eddy above.
   Nearer, the hours

are ours to make
   the most of—

or to learn,
   with practice, to relent.

Scars grow
   smaller.

So too, the future—

Rest, I said.
   Remain—

Return,
   begs the wind

circling what won't
   stay put.

My brother—not yet
born, or born

& unknown—
wanders without me,

a new moon.
Time's slow

tide, the hours
an undertow.

Even below water
you can hear him holler

as he drowns.
We cross the Sound—

The lighthouse still up
for sale.

Reefs you cannot
see—like tomorrow

or grief, a volcano's
ashen feet.

What keeps us.

Bellows breathe
on their own.

The grey
lady's beauty.

All I own.

*

Bodies are built
to fail. To fall

& only once
in a while, to rise.

Otherwise, end.

Otherwise, fade
with the light.

Other arms
will lift you up, I know,

carry you crying
to my grave.

The weeds & weather will
sing my name.

Look away.   (179)

Let them let me down
without you watching.

Sunflowers.

Their heads seek the sun—
or bend without one

even after cut—
angling in the water

toward what
brightness we borrow.

It's death there
is no cure for—

life the long
disease.

If we're lucky.

Otherwise, short
trip beyond.

And below.

Noon,
growing shadow.

I chase the quiet
round the house.

Soon the sound—

wind wills
its way against

the panes. Welcome
the rain.

Welcome
the moon's squinting

into space.
The trees

bow like priests.

The storm lifts
up the leaves.

Why not sing.

Acknowledgments

Thanks for the support of the USA James Baldwin Fellowship, a Massachusetts Cultural Arts Council grant, and a sabbatical from Emory University, without which this book couldn't have been completed. I'd also like to thank the Squaw Valley Community of Writers and the Vermont Studio Center, where several of these poems, particularly the "Book of Hours" sequence, began.

In earlier forms, the poems "Nesting" and "Teething" (as "New Year's Letter") appeared on QuickMuse.com, a website where two poets are given fifteen minutes to write from the same prompt. These and many of the titles in the "Confirmation" section (including "Lightening") are taken from the terminology of pregnancy and infancy.

"Thirst" is for Randall and Nancy Burkett, with appreciation for the ferns. Thanks to Catherine Bowman for the notion of "Beasting," mentioned in the poem of that title, which she encountered in the writing of Ted Hughes. "Lower Haight" is for Danny Rimera. "Miracle Removal" is in memoriam Helen Hill.

*

Some of these poems have appeared or are forthcoming in the following journals and magazines. Thanks to the editors for their support:

Agni: "Codicil," "Pilgrimage."

American Poetry Review: "Gravity," and three from "Book of Hours" ("Does the wind wonder," "Winter's thunder," "My brother").

American Scholar: "Sorrow," "Wintering," "Snow in April," "Effects," "Pity." "Wintering" also appears in *Best American Poetry 2013,* edited by Denise Duchamel.

The Atlantic: "Colostrum."

Boulevard Magenta (Ireland): "Gravida," "Montagne Noire," "Linea Nigra."

Georgia Review: "Lightening," "Jaundice."

Kenyon Review: "Thirst," "Greening."

Lo-Ball: "City of God," "Annunciation" ("Do not answer").

New American Writing: "Teething" ("The mouth") and "Teething" ("Son, the words that aren't") as "New Year's Letter."

New England Review: from "Book of Hours" ("How to listen").

The New Republic: "Rosetta."

The New Yorker: "Bereavement," "Crowning," "Expecting." "Expecting" also appears in *Best American Poetry 2012,* edited by Mark Doty.

Orion: Miracle Removal.

Ploughshares: "Pity," "Spring Training."

Poetry: "Pietà," "The Mission," and five poems from "Book of Hours" ("The light here leaves you," "The burnt, blurred world," "Black like an eye," "The sun's small fury," and "It's death there"). These last were later reprinted in *The Best American Poetry 2008,* edited by Charles Wright.

Progressive: "Charity."

Quickmuse (online): "Nesting," "Teething" ("The words").

Slate: "Elegy, Fathers Day," "Act Now & Save."

Tin House: "Solace," "Anniversary," "Mercy."

"Grief" (the handkerchief) first appeared as part of *Landmarks: Celebrating 40 Years of the Gallery Press,* a broadside published by the Gallery Press for the dlr Poetry Now International Poetry Festival in 2010. Thanks to Peter Fallon.

Several poems from the "Book of Hours" sequence appeared in *Breviary,* a limited fine-press edition from Sutton Hoo Press.

A NOTE ABOUT THE AUTHOR

KEVIN YOUNG is the author of seven previous books of poetry, including *Ardency: A Chronicle of the Amistad Rebels*, winner of a 2012 American Book Award, and *Jelly Roll*, a finalist for the National Book Award. He is the editor of eight other collections, most recently *The Hungry Ear: Poems of Food & Drink*. Young's book *The Grey Album: On the Blackness of Blackness* won the Graywolf Nonfiction Prize, was a *New York Times* Notable Book and a finalist for the National Book Critics Circle Award for criticism, and won the PEN Open Book Award. He is currently the Atticus Haygood Professor of Creative Writing and English, curator of Literary Collections, and curator of the Raymond Danowski Poetry Library at Emory University.

A NOTE ON THE TYPE

The text of this book was set in Bembo, a facsimile of a typeface cut by Francesco Griffo for Aldus Manutius, the celebrated Venetian printer, in 1495. The face was named for Pietro Cardinal Bembo, the author of the small treatise entitled *De Aetna* in which it first appeared. Through the research of Stanley Morison, it is now generally acknowledged that all oldstyle type designs up to the time of William Caslon can be traced to the Bembo cut. The present-day version of Bembo was introduced by the Monotype Corporation of London in 1929. Sturdy, well-balanced, and finely proportioned, Bembo is a face of rare beauty and great legibility in all of its sizes.

Composed by North Market Street Graphics,
Lancaster, Pennsylvania

Printed and bound by Berryville Graphics,
Berryville, Virginia

Designed by Cassandra J. Pappas